A FIELD GUIDE ON
GENDER AND SEXUALITY

A Field Guide on Gender and Sexuality
© 2024 by Ligonier Ministries

Published by Ligonier Ministries
421 Ligonier Court, Sanford, FL 32771
Ligonier.org

Printed in China
Amity Printing Company
0000724
First edition, second printing

ISBN 978-1-64289-644-2 (Paperback)
ISBN 978-1-64289-645-9 (ePub)

Cover design: Ligonier Creative
Interior design and typeset: Ligonier Editorial

Library of Congress Control Number: 2024933492

A FIELD GUIDE ON GENDER AND SEXUALITY

LIGONIER MINISTRIES

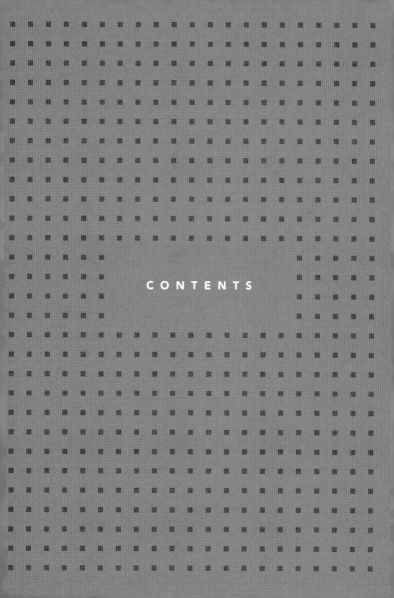

CONTENTS

I. BEING HUMAN

II. HOMOSEXUALITY AND TRANSGENDERISM

III. EVENTS AND ASSOCIATIONS

IV. THE GOSPEL AND LOVE

I.

BEING
HUMAN

. . .

THE WORLD is confused about sex, gender, and identity. Christians have a solid foundation for understanding these subjects, however, because the Bible tells us that we were created by God in His image (Gen. 1:26). Based on Scripture, this section answers questions related to what it means to be human.

QUESTIONS ANSWERED

What does it mean to be made in the image of God?

To be made in the image of God means that human beings reflect the glory, character, and rule of God in a way that other creatures do not. Therefore, we as human beings have a greater dignity than other creatures. Scripture first mentions human beings in Genesis 1, explaining that God created mankind in His image, both males and females (v. 27). The wider historical context of Genesis and the specific commands given in Genesis 1:26–28 give us the most important information for understanding what it means to be God's image bearers.

The first readers of the book of Genesis were familiar with images of the king that were used in the surrounding pagan empires. These were statues and other physical depictions of the king, who was often considered to be a god himself as well as an image of the pagan gods. These statues were set up throughout the empire to call attention to the king and to remind people of who was really in charge (e.g., Dan. 3:1–7). In light of this context, that human beings are physical images of the one true God indicates that part of what it means to bear God's image is to show creation that God is King and is to be served. Furthermore, that Scripture views all people as God's image bearers and not just the king, as in the pagan empires, shows that all people have an inherent worth and dignity because all people reflect God. Sin has marred this image, so we do not reflect God as we ought, but the image has not been lost entirely.

Looking to Genesis 1:26–28, we see that when God created males and females in His image, He also gave

"

SO GOD
CREATED MAN
IN HIS OWN IMAGE,
IN THE IMAGE
OF GOD
HE CREATED HIM;
MALE AND FEMALE
HE CREATED THEM.

GENESIS 1:27

them the command to be fruitful and multiply and to take dominion over creation. This literary context helps us understand that imaging God means that we create life and exercise rule over the created order. Because we are to point people to God, this entails ruling over creation as God would want us to reign and have dominion. We are vice-regents—lesser kings and queens who are supposed to govern creation in submission to the revealed will of the Great King, the Lord God Almighty.

Genesis 2 tells us that the first people God made, Adam and Eve, were placed in a garden and told to work and keep it. The garden of Eden was an orderly space with defined boundaries, and it could not hold many people. As Adam and Eve had children, eventually some would have to move outside the garden because there would be no room left. The commission of keeping the garden and pointing people to God, then, means that human beings were made to take the order of Eden to the rest of the world. By exercising dominion, we are to make creation even more orderly and fruitful and thus more reflective of the glory of God.

We can draw certain implications for what it means to bear God's image from these original commands. Exercising dominion and wisely governing God's resources require using reason and forming relationships with other image bearers, for dominion is a task to be shared by all people. To be made in God's image, therefore, means that we are beings with minds and wills who can think and that we are relational beings who can love others. The language of guarding and keeping Eden in Genesis 2:15 is used also of the priests of Israel in Numbers 1:53. This tells us that bearing God's image has a religious dimension; to be image bearers is to worship and serve the Creator.

Importantly, the fall into sin has damaged our capacity to bear God's image as we ought, but it has not destroyed that image entirely. Scripture tells us that after the fall into sin, people are still made in the image and "likeness of God" (James 3:9). Since we reflect the One who has the most dignity and worth, God Himself, human beings have more dignity and worth than the rest of creation (Ps. 8:1–9). Although our thinking, affections, and bodies and everything else about us have been affected by sin, we can still see the image of God in every person, though imperfectly. To know perfectly what it means to be made in God's image, we must look to the Lord Jesus Christ, "who is the image of God" (2 Cor. 4:4). Only He has lived a life that perfectly images God, and as we are conformed to Him by grace and the work of the Holy Spirit, we more and more rightly reflect God as His image bearers (2 Cor. 3:17–18).

What is sex for?

Sex is the God-created means by which a man and a woman who are joined together in a covenant marriage bond can produce offspring and enjoy exclusive relational and physical intimacy together. Sex was created by God, as recorded in Genesis 2:21–25, to carry out the creation mandate of Genesis 1:28: "Be fruitful and multiply and fill the earth and subdue it." God issued this command to man and woman, whom He created in His image as physical and relational complements to one another. Husband and wife would fulfill this mandate by uniting in a marriage union that involves sexual intercourse, through which sperm and egg unite

"

AND GOD
BLESSED THEM. AND
GOD SAID TO THEM,
"BE FRUITFUL
AND MULTIPLY
AND FILL THE EARTH
AND SUBDUE IT."

GENESIS 1:28

to form a human embryo. God's kingdom thus expands through the creation of more image bearers. There is also another important purpose for sex. God made sex for the husband and wife to enjoy one another and to fulfill within the marriage covenant the relational and sexual longings with which He created them (see Gen. 2:23).

This dual purpose of sex highlights the goodness of God's design and helps us identify erroneous views and mishandlings of the gift of sex. Sex is not intended to be a means of self-expression or self-gratification (1 Cor. 7:3–4). Since God created sex, He sets the rules for and the boundaries of sex. God doesn't sanction sex in every context; nor does He sanction every sexual act. According to the Bible, the only context in which sex is permitted is that of a covenant union between one man and one woman, which is intended to be exclusive and lifelong (Mark 10:6–9; Heb. 13:4). From the very beginning, the one-man-and-one-woman boundary is implied in the creation of only one woman for Adam (Matt. 19:4–6). God didn't create five wives for Adam, but one. God didn't create another man for Adam, but a woman. Furthermore, Adam's biology and Eve's biology are suited to one another. From their chromosomes to the shape of their reproductive organs, there is a harmonious design that God has woven into the creation of the two sexes for the purpose of fitting husband and wife together. Eve was made from Adam as equally dignified and perfectly suited to be Adam's counterpart so that together they could find satisfaction for their relational and physical desires (Gen. 2:18). She perfectly corresponded to Adam and was given the special privilege of being the helper that Adam needed to fulfill God's command to be fruitful and multiply and take dominion over creation.

As with all things that God has created, sex has the ultimate purpose of bringing Him glory, and the proper use of this gift is to glorify and enjoy God. When humans use sex in a wrongful manner, it displeases God and undermines the purposes for which He created sex. Sexual immorality also brings significant consequences because the act of sexual intercourse unites a man and a woman together physically and relationally. This is why the Apostle Paul writes: "Do you not know that he who is joined to a prostitute becomes one body with her? For, as it is written,

"

FLEE FROM
SEXUAL IMMORALITY.
EVERY OTHER SIN
A PERSON COMMITS
IS OUTSIDE THE BODY,
BUT THE SEXUALLY
IMMORAL PERSON
SINS AGAINST
HIS OWN BODY.

1 CORINTHIANS 6:18

'The two will become one flesh.' But he who is joined to the Lord becomes one spirit with him. Flee from sexual immorality. Every other sin a person commits is outside the body, but the sexually immoral person sins against his own body" (1 Cor. 6:16–18). The book of Hebrews states that the marriage bed should be undefiled (Heb. 13:4). By definition, a nonmarital sexual encounter (i.e., "bed") is defiled. Sexual activity between unmarried people—even that which does not include sexual intercourse—is the fruit of lust. Such activity is sinful and often leads to even more heinous sexual immorality. Any and all perversions of the gift of sex—including (but not limited to) pornography, homosexual activity, extramarital sex, bestiality, pedophilia, orgies, and promiscuity—are sinful practices and misuses of God's original design for sex. Nevertheless, the biblical Christian sexual ethic tells us that sex, because God created it for procreation and for the mutual enjoyment of husband and wife, is good when experienced within the proper context of marriage.

Do we create our own identities?

Yes and no. Our identities relate to the characteristics that make up who we are. In some ways we create our own identities, and in other ways we do not. We create our identities in the sense that we choose some things related to who we are. Many of these choices concern secondary matters where God gives us much freedom. For example, someone might study to be an electrician, and upon embarking on his career, he might identify as an electrician. The same can be said if a person loves a particular sports team and decides to identify as a fan, or if a person enjoys stamp collecting and chooses to identify as a stamp collector.

On the other hand, there are other identities that we don't choose; they are given to us. These are usually things that are more primary descriptors of who we are. For example, none of us chose where we were born. If someone was born in America, he might choose to hide his birthplace (for whatever reason), but he cannot escape the reality of his having been born there. The same is true of whatever family we were born into and whether we were born as a boy or a girl. We can choose to hide, suppress, or ignore the truth of these unchosen and primary identities, but they remain true because they are objective reality.

Identity is a complex subject, and our lives often involve a mixture of chosen and unchosen characteristics. For example, aspects of one's race and personality are unchosen, though we can choose to identify with these things to greater or lesser degrees. Someone who is genetically Spanish, for example, might choose to identify with Spanish culture depending on their personality and context. Or someone who is naturally analytic might choose to develop that talent and identify with being analytic—perhaps by becoming a mathematician. It's important to remember, however, that in the end, our identities involve both chosen and unchosen things. We both do and do not create our own identities. With respect to our gender, we do not choose; God does, because He created us.

For Christians, our deepest, primary identity relates to our being *in Christ*. Paul says that it is no longer we who live but Christ who lives in us (Gal. 2:20). Paul points to his union with Christ to help Christians understand that their identity as Christians is their primary identity (Rom. 6:5–11). Since being in Christ is our primary identity, Christians should make every effort to understand what it means to be in Christ.

How do we know there are only two genders? What about people who are born with ambiguous bodies?

We know that there are only two genders because that is the testimony of both special revelation, which is the Bible, and general revelation, which consists of the truths we learn about God and the world from the created world. The existence of people with ambiguous bodies does not contradict the fact that only two genders exist but rather reinforces it.

The first and most important way that we know that there are only two genders is through the Bible. The creation account states unambiguously that God created man "male and female" (Gen. 1:27), and Jesus affirms this truth (Matt. 19:4–6). The Bible never speaks of a third sex, though it speaks many times of "men and women" and "sons and daughters," and it forbids practices that could blur the distinction between the sexes (e.g., see Deut. 22:5).

Scientifically, there are only two genders as well. Reproduction for humans depends on the sex binary, as it does for other mammals. A male and a female come together to produce an offspring. There is no room in the equation for a third sex. The sex binary is part of an individual's biological makeup even down to the genetic level—the individual either has a Y chromosome, making him male, or does not, making her female. There is no ambiguity. This binary is exhibited most clearly in the difference in reproductive organs, but it is manifested in various other ways that have been recognized over the course of history and across cultures. These manifestations include differences in average size and strength and differences in secondary sex characteristics such as body hair, the Adam's apple, and other changes that come with the onset of puberty as a result of male and female sex hormones.

Sometimes individuals are born with ambiguous sex characteristics due to a variety of extremely rare conditions.

Affected individuals, often known as *intersex*, nevertheless still manifest a particular sex based on their chromosomes, even if their physical bodies are ambiguous. *Intersex* therefore doesn't imply another sex besides male and female, and these conditions thus do not overturn the existence of the sex binary. These conditions are, rather, a consequence of the fall, which affected all creation (Rom. 8:20). That we recognize intersex conditions as aberrations actually points to the reality of the sex binary. People with intersex conditions are made in the image of God, just like all other humans, and they deserve our prayers, sympathy, and support. But their conditions cannot lead us to deny the male/female binary that God created. They should be encouraged to live out their biological sex insofar as it is possible.

What should I think when someone claims to be a different gender than their biological sex?

When someone claims to be a different gender than their biological sex, we should remember that biological sex is an objective truth revealed by God. To reject the truth about how God has made us is to reject the wisdom and goodness of God, and therefore, it is to reject God Himself. People who do so, though they may hold their belief sincerely, are being deceived and need the same thing that every other sinner needs: a change of heart by the Holy Spirit (John 3:3–5; Titus 3:4–5).

People who claim to be a different gender than their biological sex often believe that some kind of mistake— either by God or by chance—resulted in a mismatch between their biological sex and the gender that they iden-tify with. They cannot be bound by what they believe to be a mistake, and they are thus free to define themselves as they see fit. This is easy for those who reject the existence of God, for in rejecting Him, they deny that they are accountable to Him and can do as they please. Yet in reality, they cannot actually deny the existence of God, for deep down they know that He exists. Rather, they are willfully choosing to suppress the knowledge of the truth to pursue their own lusts (Rom. 1:18–19, 24–25). Those who do acknowledge God's existence will respond to that knowledge in one of two ways regarding their gender. Some will seek to create a version of God in their own image, wrongly concluding

"

THE HEART IS
DECEITFUL ABOVE
ALL THINGS, AND
DESPERATELY SICK;
WHO CAN
UNDERSTAND IT?

JEREMIAH 17:9

that He supports their attempts to change their gender as a morally neutral—or even praiseworthy—endeavor. The prophet Isaiah condemns such moral maneuvering when he says, "Woe to those who call evil good and good evil" (Isa. 5:20). Others will acknowledge that they are rebelling against God but willfully choose to defy Him anyway.

Many people who claim to be another gender sincerely believe it to be true. Yet such beliefs, however sincere they may be, are wrong. Jeremiah 17:9 shows us the deception, twistedness, and corruption of the human heart: "The heart is deceitful above all things, and desperately sick; who can understand it?" People who make such claims are being led astray into sin and error because the moral compass of their hearts is pointing them in the wrong direction. Though Christians are to have great compassion on fellow image bearers who have been twisted by the sin and suffering that is present in a fallen world, we must never believe that God has made a mistake in how He created each of us, nor can we ever conclude that God looks favorably on our rejection of His Word and will.

Further, we must remember the Apostle Paul's words to Titus: "For we ourselves were once foolish, disobedient, led astray, slaves to various passions and pleasures, passing our days in malice and envy, hated by others and hating one another" (Titus 3:3). The people we encounter who claim to be a different gender have been led astray, as we all were in various ways before God saved us. Thus, their only hope and ours is the mercy of God in regenerating our hearts and giving us eyes to see Him and ourselves as we truly are.

Does gender reassignment or affirmation surgery actually make someone a different sex?

No, gender reassignment or affirmation surgery does not actually make someone a different sex. Biological sex is a fixed reality that cannot be changed through surgical intervention or other means. Gender cannot actually be reassigned because the sex chromosomes that we are born with cannot be changed. Plastic surgery and hormones can make cosmetic changes to the body and thus create a simulation of masculine or feminine features, but they cannot change one's fundamental biology.

Some argue that such interventions do not change one's sex but merely alter the external markers of sex to match the person's internal sense of gender. For instance, a biological male might say that he is actually female regardless of the sex characteristics he possesses, and therefore, interventions such as hormone therapy and surgery do not change the person from male to female; he was always female. Advocates of these interventions thus sometimes prefer the term *gender affirmation*. This argument is erroneous and must be rejected. History, biology, Scripture, and common sense tell us that there are only two sexes and that one's sex cannot be changed.

Is there a difference between one's sex and gender?

The answer depends on how the terms are used. *Sex* has traditionally referred to one's biology—whether one is born with male or female genitalia and whether one has X or Y chromosomes, for example. *Gender*, however, has come to mean how one expresses or feels about his or her sex as male or female. The problem is that, especially in liberal academic circles, sex eventually came to be completely divorced from gender, so that today it's normal to hear people talk about being a transgender woman (a biological man who identifies as a woman) or transgender man (a biological woman who identifies as a man). LGBTQ people would, of course, deny that they are merely performing or feeling something and insist that their gender goes deeper—it expresses who they really are, regardless of their biological sex.

Christians, on the other hand, believe that our biological sex is who we are, because both Scripture and the created world testify that God gave us our sexual identity when He created our bodies as male or female (Gen. 1:27). Therefore, our biological sex *is* our gender. That's not to deny that men and women express their maleness and femaleness in a multitude of ways in various cultures around the world—in clothing, speech, family rituals, and so on. But regardless of our culture, it's our responsibility to steward our bodies according to their maleness or femaleness. God's Word has much to say about how we must live as a man or woman in any culture (Prov. 1; Col. 3:18–25; Eph. 5:22–33). We cannot redefine reality simply by acting in a different way, by going through selective surgeries, or by taking hormones that ultimately cannot alter our chromosomes or our body's natural disposition.

II.

HOMOSEXUALITY
AND
TRANSGENDERISM

■ ■ ■

THE RAPIDLY growing acceptance of LGBTQ lifestyles has made it increasingly important that Christians be prepared to give an adequate response (1 Peter 3:15). Based on the Bible, this section answers questions related to homosexuality and transgenderism.

QUESTIONS ANSWERED

Is same-sex attraction a sin?

Yes, same-sex attraction is a sin. In the Sermon on the Mount, Jesus makes plain that the desire for sin is itself sin. For instance, He says that to look on another person with lust is to break the commandment against adultery even if the physical act of adultery does not take place (Matt. 5:27–30). It is, of course, worse to commit the act of adultery than it is to have the desire alone, but having the desire still violates the seventh commandment.

Many passages in Scripture tell us, moreover, that same-sex sexual acts are sin. Same-sex sexual acts go against God's natural design for human beings, which is that one man and one woman join together in marriage and engage in sexual activity for the purposes of bearing children and strengthening the marital union (Gen. 1–2). Same-sex sexual acts cannot fulfill these purposes. Furthermore, other passages such as Romans 1:26–27 and 1 Corinthians 6:9–10 tell us that same-sex sexual acts are wicked and will incur the eternal judgment of God if a person never turns from them and trusts in Christ alone for salvation. Since same-sex sexual behavior is sinful, and since the desire for sin is sin, then the presence of same-sex attraction and its attendant same-sex sexual desires is sin.

Some people have said that same-sex sexual attraction and desires must be from God because He is the Creator, and since God does not make mistakes, these desires and attractions must be good and should therefore be expressed in physical acts. While it is true that God is the Creator of all things, Scripture tells us explicitly that sin does not come from the hand of God in any direct way. "God cannot be tempted with evil, and he himself tempts

"

GOD CANNOT

BE TEMPTED

WITH EVIL,

AND HE HIMSELF

TEMPTS NO ONE.

JAMES 1:13

no one" (James 1:13). Because God is sovereign and works out all things according to His will (Eph. 1:11), we must say that the Lord ordains that some people will experience same-sex attraction and desires, but He does so in such a way that He Himself does not give the desires and cannot be blamed for people's sinful desires. Sinful desires are not good in themselves, and they come from our own sinful hearts, not from God (James 1:14).

Yet God does give to those who trust in Him the will and the power to fight our sinful desires as we work out our "salvation with fear and trembling" (Phil. 2:12). He gives us new hearts that desire the good things He has made. He has also given us the Holy Spirit to empower us and the church to assist us as we seek to be conformed more and more to the image of God in Christ. God allows us to experience sinful desires without giving them to us directly, and He allows this so that we might work against those desires, by His Spirit, for our ultimate good and His ultimate glory (Rom. 8:28).

What's the difference between same-sex attraction and same-sex sexual behavior?

Same-sex attraction is the internal desire for a sexual relationship with another person of the same sex, while same-sex sexual behavior constitutes physical sexual acts between two or more persons of the same sex. The desire for same-sex sexual behavior may arise from an internal temptation or an external temptation. The desire is sinful in itself, but the sin is compounded when a person succumbs to temptation and the desire comes to expression in physical acts (James 1:14–15).

Human beings experience temptation both externally and internally. An external temptation occurs when something sinful outside our hearts and minds is presented as an option for us to engage in. Our hearts may respond to this external temptation to sin by desiring the sin, or they may find it unappealing or may immediately reject the temptation without ever desiring it. An example of an external temptation would be when the devil tempted Jesus. The devil presented Jesus with the option of receiving dominion over all the kingdoms of the world by worshiping him, but Jesus rejected him, never desiring to worship Satan in any way (Matt. 4:8–10). Another example of an external temptation would be a friend's asking you to join him in stealing a car when you have not thought of the idea. Being presented with such a temptation in itself would not be a sin for you, but to join the friend or to desire to steal would be a sin.

Internal temptations are those temptations that arise within our own hearts and minds and require no external encouragement, though sometimes an internal temptation occurs in response to an experience with the external world. For example, a married man might see a beautiful woman who is not his wife and recognize her beauty in his heart or mind. Such recognition is not in itself sinful. The man's heart and mind, however, might take that recognition, dwell on it, and come to desire sexual intimacy with that woman even if he never acts on it. At that point, the recognition of beauty has transformed into an internal sexual temptation and an internal sexual desire, which is sinful because it is a desire to commit adultery.

Human beings are called to live according to godly desires shaped by Scripture and to seek the renewal of their minds by the Word of God so that they can develop godly thoughts and desires and say no to ungodly thoughts and desires (Rom. 6:13–16; 12:1–2). It is a grosser violation of God's law to let any sinful desire, including same-sex sexual desire, come to expression in physical acts than to have that desire remain internal. To give in to temptation instead of resisting and rejecting it, even if that means only developing or nurturing an internal desire for sin, still breaks the law of God, but acting on same-sex attraction by committing a sex act of any kind with another person of the same sex compounds our guilt.

What's the difference between gender dysphoria and transgenderism?

Gender dysphoria describes a sense of unease or distress that results from an incongruity between a person's biological sex and his or her psychological sense of gender (commonly referred to as *gender identity*). *Transgender* typically describes people who choose to live in a manner that does not correspond to their biological sex. As we interact with people, it's important to recognize the difference between gender dysphoria and transgenderism because not everyone who experiences gender dysphoria adopts a transgender lifestyle.

Gender dysphoria sometimes involves a person's desiring to be the other gender, attain the characteristics of the other gender, or be treated as the other gender. Thus, gender dysphoria lies in the domain of a person's desires and preferences, but it doesn't necessarily result in actions taken to identify as or attempt to be another gender.

Transgenderism, on the other hand, more commonly involves people's choosing to live as a male despite being born female or as a female despite being born male. Transgender people may or may not experience gender dysphoria. This willful choice to live as a gender that is different from their biological sex may result in "gender affirmation" pursuits such as changing one's name or pronouns, taking hormone therapy, or getting surgery in an attempt to "create" or remove sex organs.

Transgenderism can often be difficult to define since proponents sometimes argue that someone's gender expression (the outward manifestation of a person's gender) doesn't need to match his or her gender identity (a person's inner psychological sense of their gender). Further, transgender people may not identify with any gender at all, may claim to be a gender other than male or female, or may blend elements of manhood and womanhood together. Such people are often called *nonbinary* or *genderqueer*.

Amid this confusion, the simplest way to distinguish gender dysphoria and transgenderism is to say that gender dysphoria relates to *desires and feelings* that people experience but do not necessarily act on, while transgenderism culminates in *actions and behaviors* that a person takes to depart from or reject his or her biological sex. By way of comparison, we might say that those who experience gender dysphoria are, in some senses, similar to those who experience same-sex attraction, while those who embrace transgenderism are, in some senses, similar to those who embrace homosexuality as an identity and in their actions.

"

PUT ON THE
NEW SELF,
CREATED AFTER
THE LIKENESS
OF GOD IN TRUE
RIGHTEOUSNESS
AND HOLINESS.

EPHESIANS 4:24

Transgender people who receive the gospel and trust in Christ will need to "put off" the actions, behaviors, and desires associated with living in a way that is inconsistent with their biological sex. Those who have come to Christ are commanded: "Put off your *old self*, which belongs to your *former manner of life* and is corrupt through *deceitful desires*, and to be *renewed in the spirit of your minds*, and to put on the *new self*, created after the likeness of God in *true righteousness and holiness*" (Eph. 4:22–24, emphasis added).

Believers who experience gender dysphoria may or may not continue to experience some level of that condition, but they can continue to grow in Christlikeness for the glory of God and the good of their neighbors, trusting the Holy Spirit to mortify lingering sinful desires. All believers are to fight the various kinds of evil desires that arise within us, and Christians who wrestle with gender dysphoria will do so as well as they seek to "put to death therefore what is earthly in [them]: sexual immorality, impurity, passion, evil desire, and covetousness, which is idolatry" (Col. 3:5).

Is it OK to call yourself a "gay Christian"?

No, believers should not call themselves "gay Christians" because the term *gay* is not neutral in our culture. While some may see *gay* as merely shorthand for experiencing same-sex attraction, the term is not simply descriptive but often indicates affirmation of sinful desires and practices. Furthermore, and more importantly, it is inappropriate for Christians to place a marker of a sinful identity alongside their new identity in Christ, as if that marker defines them as much as being in Christ defines them (1 Cor. 6:11). Christians, after all, are new creations in Christ (2 Cor. 5:17). To define ourselves by our sinful desires calls into question the reality that we have been re-created for holiness in Christ. It also implies that Christ Himself approves of sin, but this is impossible (see Gal. 2:17). Thus, Christians should not use terms such as "gay Christian" to describe themselves because doing so bears false witness to Christ and His work. No act of sin or desire for sin is fundamental to a Christian's identity.

Is homosexual sin worse than other sins?

Yes. Homosexual sin is contrary to God's fundamental design in creation and therefore worse than many other sins. Some Christians believe that all sins are equal, but this is not the case. Scripture teaches that every sin is worthy of damnation but that some sins incur a harsher judgment from God because of various factors. In one of His parables, Jesus makes the observation that when servants do not do the will of the master, the one who knew the master's will but did not do it receives a harsher punishment than the one who did not know the master's will (Luke 12:41–48). Both are punished, but one is punished more severely. Jesus says in John 19:11 that the men who handed Jesus over to Pontius Pilate committed a "greater sin" than Pilate himself.

Homosexual sin is particularly severe because of its perversion of God's design for creation. Homosexual sin is more scandalous than other sins because it is a departure from God's creational design and standards for sex. Homosexuality—whether between a man and a man or a woman and a woman—constitutes one of the deepest levels of depravity, degeneracy, and rebellion. In Romans 1, the Apostle Paul

"

FOR THIS REASON
GOD GAVE THEM UP
TO DISHONORABLE
PASSIONS. FOR THEIR
WOMEN EXCHANGED
NATURAL RELATIONS
FOR THOSE THAT
ARE CONTRARY
TO NATURE;

AND THE MEN
LIKEWISE
GAVE UP NATURAL
RELATIONS . . .
RECEIVING IN
THEMSELVES THE
DUE PENALTY
FOR THEIR ERROR.

ROMANS 1:26–27

"

shows how God gave mankind over to a deeper depravity for their suppression of the truth (v. 18), their ingratitude (v. 21), and their idolatry (v. 23). The deeper and more heinous depravity that God gave mankind over to is *homosexuality*. Paul writes: "For this reason God gave them up to dishonorable passions. For their women exchanged natural relations for those that are contrary to nature; and the men likewise gave up natural relations with women and were consumed with passion for one another, men committing shameless acts with men and receiving in themselves the due penalty for their error" (vv. 26–27). Homosexuality is described here as *dishonorable, contrary to nature, passionate, shameless, punishable,* and *erroneous*. It is described in such harsh terms because it is especially rebellious against God and because it is contrary to the natural order of things. Heterosexual sin, on the other hand, though it, too, is evil, is not contrary to nature. Homosexuality denies the reality that man is made for woman and woman for man. It is a significant rejection of the natural order that God has created and constitutes a flagrant disregard for God and His purposes for sex.

Yet we must remember that while homosexual sin is a severe sin, it is not the unforgivable sin (Luke 12:10). All who turn to Christ in true faith and repentance will be forgiven, no matter the sin they have committed. Sinners of all kinds, including those who have committed homosexual sin, have found forgiveness in Christ.

Can Christians with same-sex attraction expect their desires to change as they grow in sanctification?

Yes, Christians who experience same-sex attraction can expect their desires to change as they grow in sanctification, though the degree and rate of change will not necessarily be uniform for all such believers. God's Word holds out this great promise for all believers: "And we all, with unveiled face, beholding the glory of the Lord, are being transformed into the same image from one degree of glory to another. For this comes from the Lord who is the Spirit" (2 Cor. 3:18). This passage teaches us that as we grow in the grace and knowledge of our Lord Jesus Christ, we become more like Him over the course of our lives. Therefore, Christians

"

AND WE ALL,
WITH UNVEILED
FACE, BEHOLDING
THE GLORY OF THE
LORD, ARE BEING
TRANSFORMED
INTO THE SAME
IMAGE

FROM ONE
DEGREE OF GLORY
TO ANOTHER.
FOR THIS COMES
FROM THE LORD WHO
IS THE SPIRIT.

2 CORINTHIANS 3:18

"

who experience same-sex attraction can expect all of their desires to change over time.

All believers—including Christians who experience same-sex attraction—can expect their desires to change as they grow in Christlikeness. For example, they can expect to grow in greater love for God and greater love for their neighbors. They can expect to hate their sin more and more. They can expect to grow in purity of heart and mind and to grow in resisting temptation (2 Peter 3:18). They can expect to increasingly display the fruit of the Spirit (Gal. 5:22–23) and to use their spiritual gifts for the upbuilding of the church. In sum, they can expect to become mature, godly men and women who disciple others in the faith and witness to the world.

Yet such growth in grace does not guarantee that all Christians who experience same-sex attraction will reach a point at which they no longer experience these desires at all. Knowing this can help believers by not setting up a false expectation of the eradication of all same-sex attraction in this life, which can lead to undue shame when they faithfully seek to live for God but find that their attraction hasn't completely gone away or has not transferred to the opposite sex to the degree that they might hope for. The road of sanctification is both the same and different for each believer. It is the same in that we are aiming at the same goal and depending on the same Spirit. It is different in that not every Christian experiences change in the exact same way or at the exact same rate. This is true with respect to every sin and not just same-sex attraction. Our goal should be to mortify all sinful desires (Rom. 8:13; Col. 3:5). Yet we understand that it will not be until the Lord Jesus returns that all our sinful desires will be put to death (Rom. 7:14–25).

Christians who experience same-sex attraction need encouragement from other brothers and sisters in Christ, especially when their unnatural attractions don't die easily. Putting sin to death is hard, but the Lord is working in us "to will and to work for his good pleasure" (Phil. 2:12–13). God has called all Christians to glorify Him and to display the all-sufficiency of His Son in their lives through seeking to mortify their desires, pursue righteousness, and trust Him with the outcome. God promises great eternal rewards to those who hold fast to Him and live to honor Him. Their hope, and ours, is that they will one day be fully restored in glorified bodies in the new heavens and earth (Rom. 8:20–24; 2 Peter 3:13). For all eternity, they will live with unspeakable joy and have perfectly ordered affections and desires as they glorify God and enjoy Him forever.

What does repentance look like for a transgender person?

Transgender is somewhat of a catchall term, but it roughly means expressing a gender identity—an internal sense of one's maleness or femaleness—that is different from one's biological sex. It could be that a biological male claims to be female or that a biological female claims to have no gender at all. Because transgender individuals are still human beings, most aspects of repentance for them will look the same as they do for non-transgender individuals. Repentance involves a true sorrow over sin, a turning from that sin unto Christ in faith, and a sincere resolve to walk in obedience to God. The specific nature of transgenderism means that repentance will involve seeking to live according to one's biological sex. This means no longer claiming to be or acting like anything other than one's biological sex. If someone is born female, for example, she should stop claiming to be male, wearing men's clothing, using male pronouns, and so on. For transgender individuals who have had gender reassignment surgery, it may not be possible to detransition surgically, for financial or medical reasons. But other options, including adjusting hormone therapy, may be possible.

III.

EVENTS
AND
ASSOCIATIONS

． ． ．

CHRISTIANS HAVE relationships with all sorts of people
and are invited to attend and participate in various kinds
of events. This section answers questions related to how
we might make decisions about what to participate in as
we strive to remain in the world while not being of the
world (John 17:14–15).

QUESTIONS
ANSWERED

Can I attend a gay wedding?

No, a Christian may not attend a gay wedding. To attend a gay wedding is to participate in an event that is an unfruitful work of darkness because it is an event that by its very nature approves of and commemorates that which is against God's law. Christians are not to take part in such evil works but are to expose them as sin and darkness (Eph. 5:5–14). Secondarily, whether or not we voice our objection to the relationship being celebrated at the ceremony, our presence at a wedding signals that we approve of the relationship. Christians may not approve of such a relationship or even give an impression of approval because marriage was instituted by God as the union of one man and one woman (Gen. 2:18–25). Our presence can therefore lead others astray.

Wedding ceremonies have several functions, including the official recognition of the legitimacy of the marriage union, the celebration of this union, and the gathering of witnesses who will encourage the couple to remain faithful to one another and their marriage vows until they are parted by death. These functions are evident in the public nature of the ceremony and in the ceremony's call for any objections to the marriage to be voiced by those in attendance. Any person who attends a wedding ceremony is engaging in a public act that declares the relationship legitimate, that celebrates the actual marital union taking place, and that makes attendees witnesses who commit themselves to hold the couple accountable to follow through on their vows. Thus, a wedding ceremony is unlike other special occasions such as a graduation party or a birthday party. Even in a secular setting, such as before a judge, a wedding is a religious act for the Christian, because we know that God created marriage as a good gift for human beings, and we cannot help but celebrate the gift and its Giver.

Because of what a marriage is and because of what a wedding is, Christians may not attend any wedding ceremony that is not for the purpose of lawfully joining one man and one woman. Many different kinds of wedding ceremonies, therefore, are inappropriate for a Christian to attend, including a gay wedding. Even if the Christian tells the couple that he or she does not support the marriage, the mere presence of the believer there, especially when he or she raises no objections during the ceremony, is an act approving of the union. Furthermore, other attendees will take the Christian's presence as a sign of his or her endorsement of the union. Since "gay marriage" is ultimately a fiction and a significant rejection of the natural order that God has instituted, the wedding cannot actually recognize the marriage as legitimate, so the ceremony is pointless as well as a mockery of the Lord and His law. Christians cannot hold a gay couple accountable to remain faithful to one another because homosexuality is a sin, the relationship itself is sinful, and it should never have been entered into.

"

TAKE NO PART
IN THE UNFRUITFUL
WORKS OF
DARKNESS,
BUT INSTEAD
EXPOSE THEM.

EPHESIANS 5:11

Christians cannot attend a gay wedding or celebrate the marriage by using their talents to celebrate the union. This means that Christian bakers cannot bake a wedding cake for a gay wedding, Christian florists cannot arrange flowers for a gay wedding, Christian artists cannot design wedding invitations for a gay wedding, and so on. Christians cannot take part in the unfruitful works of darkness (Eph. 5:11), and a gay wedding is such a work of darkness because it holds up a forbidden relationship as something that should be celebrated.

Can I attend the wedding of non-Christians? A Christian to a non-Christian? Cohabiting people? Someone who's had an unbiblical divorce?

Whether a Christian can attend a wedding depends on the nature of the wedding. In brief, attending a wedding indicates that the attendee approves of the union. It means that the attendee believes the union is a good thing and that there is no reason to object to the marriage's going forward.

Marriage is a creation ordinance given to all humanity when God made the world (Gen. 2:24). It is for all mankind, not merely for Christians. It is lawful for all kinds of people to marry, as long as the union is between one man and one woman. Therefore, there is no reason to object to non-Christians' getting married to one another. A Christian can freely attend such a wedding.

The situation is different for a wedding between a Christian and a non-Christian. God permits Christians to marry only other Christians (1 Cor. 7:39), so it is unlawful for a Christian to marry a non-Christian. We should therefore avoid giving tacit approval to such a union by attending the wedding. This may be more challenging when the Christian is a family member, but we can still love and care for a fellow believer without approving of his or her unbiblical marriage to a non-Christian. Furthermore, Christians should not date or court non-Christians, since such relationships are intended to eventually lead to marriage and may put Christians in a position to sin in the meantime.

People who are cohabiting are clearly in sin. If the man and woman are professing Christians and members of a church, the church and presiding minister should be the first to call them to repentance. It is better, however, for them to marry than to continue in that sin. Ideally, they would separate before the wedding, but their failure to do so does not make the union illegitimate. The marriage is still between one man and one woman and, therefore, categorically different from the question of an LGBTQ wedding.

Whether someone has had an unbiblical divorce is not entirely up to the individual Christian's judgment. It is the purview of the church to determine whether someone is the innocent party in a divorce. If the church judges that someone is the innocent party, that person is free to remarry, and a Christian may freely attend the wedding. If the church has determined that the person is not innocent, then the Christian should not attend the wedding, as it is illegitimate and should not go forward. If no determination has been made, then it is a matter of conscience. If a Christian could not attend the wedding in good conscience, then he or she should not attend.

Isn't it more loving to attend a wedding even if we disagree with the participants' lifestyle?

No. Because love is always rooted in the truth, it is not more loving to attend a wedding even if we disagree with the participants' lifestyle.

Ephesians 4:15 tells us that we are to be people who are known for "speaking the truth in love." Often we think this means that we must be gracious in our speech, and no doubt that is required (Col. 4:6). Yet graciousness in speech does not exhaust what it means to speak the truth in love. To speak the truth in love requires us to speak the truth as God defines it and to exercise love as God defines it. We should not be cruel when we verbally communicate our biblically based disagreement with a person's lifestyle, always telling them that God will forgive them if they trust in Christ alone and turn from their sin. Nevertheless, the loving act is not to verbally approve of sin. In fact, it is most unloving to communicate such approval, for we know that impenitent sins of many kinds, including sexual sin, will prevent entrance to the kingdom of God (1 Cor. 6:9–10). People need to know that persistent impenitence is the

"

DO YOU
NOT KNOW THAT
THE UNRIGHTEOUS
WILL NOT INHERIT
THE KINGDOM
OF GOD?

1 CORINTHIANS 6:9

road to hell. Nothing could be more loving than warning people of eternal judgment and calling them to escape it by faith in Christ.

Furthermore, we communicate not only with our words but also with our actions. We can tell a couple again and again that we do not agree with their sinful lifestyle, but by attending a wedding we are communicating that we approve of the marriage or at least that our concerns about it are not very serious. Other attendees will also perceive our attending such a wedding as an approval unless we tell all of them that we disagree with the lifestyle. Even then, our actions call our convictions into question. Our attendance will be confusing to the attendees and harmful to the communication of the truth that the lifestyle in question is damnable. It is more loving to communicate clearly and consistently than it is to leave room for doubt about God's hatred of a particular sin or the basis or strength of our convictions. The most loving thing that we can do in such a situation is to not attend a wedding. We do not have to reject the invitation with undue harshness, but the clear communication of truth and authentic love requires that we not attend the ceremony or reception.

Is it OK to use people's preferred pronouns?

No, a Christian should not intentionally use a person's preferred pronouns if those pronouns clearly do not reflect the person's biological sex.

The phenomenon of preferred pronouns is relatively new but didn't develop in a vacuum. In the last few hundred years in Western culture, there has been an ideological shift regarding how human beings think about our identity. The culture has come to regard our feelings as determinative and now regards our bodies as nearly irrelevant to our identity. Significantly, who we *feel* we are subjectively has taken priority over who we are objectively. Feelings are more important than reality. Who or what a person's mind says he is takes precedence over who or what he actually is. This has led to the trend of people's adopting pronouns that don't match their biological sex simply because they *feel* different from their bodies. In turn, the expectation has become that all people must appreciate and respect those pronouns regardless of whether those pronouns reflect reality.

Words have meaning. Our words can convey truth, or they can convey lies. Truth cannot be upheld when language and words are detached from reality. The use of pronouns that are contrary to one's biological sex is not merely a trivial matter of empty words. Often, the demand for the use of preferred pronouns is promoted as loving and empathetic. The thought is that since the words don't harm us, why can't we refer to a male as "she" and a female as "he" if that is what they prefer? At first glance, this might seem like sensible reasoning. But behind the demand to use certain language is the greater demand to compromise on truth and reality—truth and reality that belong to God. The Christian cannot in good conscience, out of love for God and love for others, affirm the ideology that our bodies are somehow distinct from who we really are as image bearers. God has made mankind male and female. To be human is to be made in the image of God with a physically gendered body and a soul. We cannot implicitly or explicitly deny how God has made human beings and what it means to be made in His image.

Proper names (e.g., Campbell, Kennedy, Leslie, Reagan, Robin, Taylor, Terry), on the other hand, are more arbitrary than pronouns. Christians must exercise wisdom and discernment when people request to be addressed by a proper name that may appear inconsistent with their biological sex. But pronouns are sex-specific, so to intentionally use pronouns that plainly do not reflect the biological sex of the individual requires adopting a view of mankind that is antithetical to the Bible's view of mankind. In addition, conveying lies by our actions or speech is never genuinely loving or compassionate. True love speaks the truth, and intentionally using inaccurate pronouns is never truthful and, therefore, never loving.

How do we know whether something is a matter of conscience or a clear teaching of Scripture?

Something is a matter of conscience when it is not forbidden by Scripture explicitly or not forbidden implicitly by good and necessary deductions from Scripture. The question of when we are free to act according to conscience is relevant in relation to contemporary issues such as gay weddings, which some argue are not forbidden in Scripture and therefore are permissible for Christians to attend.

Christians sometimes disagree with one another regarding what is permissible (Rom. 14:1–15:7). The disagreement might be over a matter of conscience, meaning that the act in question may or may not be acceptable depending on the individual. Or the disagreement might be over a clear teaching of Scripture, meaning that it applies to all Christians. In other words, some things are inherently wrong and to be avoided by all believers while other things might be wrong for one person but permissible for another.

Paul addressed this matter using the example of meat sacrificed to idols in Romans 14 and 1 Corinthians 8–10. In the first-century Roman Empire, most people were pagans and offered sacrifices to pagan gods. Often, any leftover meat from those sacrifices was sold in the marketplace as food. Some Christians thought that it was wrong to eat such meat because of its association with pagan worship, but others thought that it was acceptable to eat the meat. This led to many disagreements in the church.

Paul noted that the meat itself was not unclean simply because it was left over from a pagan ritual. Christians could freely eat of it without sinning as long as they were convinced that it was not inherently unclean. Believers who were convinced that the meat was unclean because of the association with paganism, however, could not eat the meat without sinning. This was because they were intentionally violating what they thought to be God's law. They may have been wrong that the meat was unclean, but once they thought it was, to eat it was to display an attitude of rejecting God's law. That attitude was the sin, not the consumption of the meat itself. In a non-Christian setting, Paul told the Christian not to eat such meat when the host of a meal told the believer that the meat was left over from a pagan sacrifice, presumably because it might lead the non-Christian to think that pagan worship was not offensive to God. Finally, Paul told Christians that they could not eat the meat if eating such meat was a part of their own participation in a pagan religious ceremony. After all, such participation is idolatrous worship. Christians were sometimes asked to participate in such ceremonies as part of the requirements for their social lives and occupations in the first century.

In light of Paul's instruction and the overall teaching of Scripture, we may discern some principles for determining if something is a matter of conscience or if it is wrong for everyone. First, anything that breaks an explicit commandment of God is wrong for all Christians. A Christian may never steal because God says, "You shall not steal" (Ex. 20:15). Second, anything that breaks a necessary implication of an explicit commandment is wrong for all Christians. A Christian may never view pornography, and we conclude this by making deductions from what He has explicitly said. God says, "You shall not commit adultery" (Ex. 20:14), and Jesus says that lustful looks constitute adultery (Matt. 5:27–30). Pornography incites lust, and it is therefore forbidden to all Christians.

If something does not break an explicit command from God or an implicit deduction from an explicit command, then it is a matter of conscience. Consider movies, for instance. All pornographic movies are forbidden to Christians, but other movies may not be. If a person thinks watching movies is a waste of time or sinful, he should not watch movies, but if a person thinks watching movies is a legitimate way to relax or enjoy God's good gifts, then he may. Neither person should seek to impose his view on the other.

Finally, there may be some cases when it is unclear if the matter is a matter of conscience or a clear teaching of God's Word. In such cases, it is wise for the Christian not to participate lest he end up breaking a commandment unwittingly. God has also given Christians pastors and elders in the local church to help direct them to Scripture and to give them wisdom regarding cases of conscience on matters that may be more difficult to discern.

Can I be friends with homosexual and transgender people?

It depends. The answer to this question is complicated, because a *friend* can sometimes refer to someone who is simply more than an acquaintance, but it can also refer to someone with whom we have a deep and abiding relationship.

Christians can be friends with homosexual and transgender people in the sense that we can and must be friendly toward them. We may even share certain interests, such as a particular hobby, or certain experiences, such as being employed in the same workplace or being students in the same class. Almost inevitably, we will find ourselves in work or social situations where we will encounter homosexual or transgender individuals. We will get to know them better than people who are complete strangers to us, and we can provide practical help to them in many ways. This kind of friendship is really the outworking of our call to be good neighbors to all people (Luke 10:25–37) and to do good to everyone as we have the opportunity (Gal. 6:10). Moreover, throughout Christian history, believers have befriended sinners of many different kinds in order to share the gospel with them. Paul and many other Christian missionaries encountered all kinds of sinful lifestyles in their journeys; their mission field was among sinners (1 Cor. 5:10). We are likewise called to preach the gospel and love our neighbors as ourselves as we seek out the lost by the grace of God.

In light of the broader biblical teaching on friendship, however, perhaps it would be better to say that our call is to be good neighbors to homosexual and transgender people. Wisdom is necessary when determining the appropriate depth of neighborliness, especially for Christian parents who are seeking to teach their children godliness. Depending on the age of the children, it might be wise to limit the children's contact with particular individuals. Christians must use their discernment in regard to their own friendships with non-Christians but also in regard to helping their children have a biblical understanding of sin and their engagement with the world.

If we are looking at what Scripture says about friendship as a relationship in which people share a close, enduring bond grounded in a common worldview and moral principles, then Christians cannot be friends with homosexual and transgender people or with any other non-Christian. Scripture paints a picture of true friendship in figures such as David and Jonathan, who covenanted to look out for each other's spiritual and physical welfare (1 Sam. 18:1–5). Non-Christians, including homosexual and transgender people, are unable to look out for our spiritual welfare because, in not following Jesus, they cannot know what spiritual welfare looks like. True friends share faith in the same God, as in the example of Ruth and Naomi (Ruth 1:6–18). Homosexuals, transgender people, and other non-Christians do not worship the one true God, so they will not be able to have deep and abiding friendships with Christians because the truth abides in us, and we must expose unfruitful works of darkness (Eph. 5:11; 2 John 1:2). A true friend will receive godly correction from us (Prov. 27:6), but unless the other person is a believer in Jesus, such correction will fall on deaf ears. This rules out deep and abiding friendship in the biblical sense with homosexuals, transgender people, and other non-Christians.

Non-Christians, including homosexuals and transgender people, will in some way take part in or approve of lifestyles that Christians cannot imitate or celebrate (2 Cor. 6:14; Eph. 5:11). Therefore, there will be limits to how deep our friendship with such people can go. It is true that Jesus

"

FAITHFUL

ARE THE WOUNDS

OF A FRIEND.

PROVERBS 27:6

was known as a "friend of . . . sinners" (Matt. 11:19), but He had deep relationships only with His disciples. He was friendly to sinners inasmuch as He did not shun them entirely and was willing to receive them as disciples and friends if they repented. Nevertheless, even as He dined with them, He never joined in or approved of their sin. We can be likewise friendly to all kinds of non-Christians, homosexuals and transgender people included, but we cannot enjoy them as true friends unless they turn from their sin and embrace Jesus Christ.

When should a Christian disassociate from someone?

An individual Christian should disassociate from someone who inevitably entices the Christian to sin or is otherwise a danger to the believer, and the church should disassociate from false teachers and impenitent sinners who profess to be Christians (1 Cor. 5:9–13).

In our lives, we are inevitably forced to make decisions about who we will associate with and the depth of each relationship we will have with others. More particularly,

Christians have to make decisions about how they associate with those who profess to be believers in Christ and with those who do not.

With respect to those who do not profess to be Christians, the answer is somewhat easier. The Bible does not demand that we withdraw from the non-Christian world entirely or cut off all relationships with those who do not believe in Jesus. Christ's command that His church make disciples of all nations (Matt. 28:18–20), for example, requires us to be in contact with both believers and nonbelievers.

In 1 Corinthians 5, we find principles for discerning when we should disassociate from someone. Paul tells us that ordinarily, individual Christians are not supposed to disassociate from those who do not claim to be believers (vv. 9–10). There may, of course, be cases where it is wise not to associate with certain unbelievers, such as when doing so will put a Christian in a place of overwhelming temptation to some kind of sin. For the most part, however, we are to have relationships with non-Christians. Even the church collectively should have such relationships

"

I WROTE TO YOU
IN MY LETTER
NOT TO ASSOCIATE WITH
SEXUALLY IMMORAL
PEOPLE—NOT AT ALL
MEANING THE SEXUALLY
IMMORAL OF THIS WORLD
. . . SINCE THEN YOU
WOULD NEED TO GO OUT
OF THE WORLD.

1 CORINTHIANS 5:9–10

when appropriate. A good relationship with the local city council, for instance, helps the church extend mercy ministry to the local community.

When we are talking about relationships with professing Christians, however, things become more complicated. Paul also tells the church in 1 Corinthians 5 to excommunicate a man who was involved in a sexual relationship with his father's wife. This man was a professing Christian but was living an incestuous lifestyle, a severe public sin that threatened the holiness of the church and called into question the truth of his profession of faith. To keep this man's persistent refusal to repent from leading others astray, he was to be put out of the church.

Paul's instructions in 1 Corinthians 5 apply Jesus' teaching on church discipline to a particular situation. Matthew 18:15–20 records our Lord's instruction on what to do about sin in the church, outlining a process of confronting the sinner in the hopes that he will repent. The goal is to prompt the sinner to turn from his wickedness. If he repents, he is to be restored to fellowship, but if he persistently refuses to repent, he is to be treated "as a Gentile and a tax collector" (v. 17). In other words, when a pro-fessing Christian is confronted over serious sin in his life and he repeatedly refuses to repent, the church is to treat him as a non-Christian. This does not mean shunning him entirely or cutting off all contact (unless the person is a serious threat to the church body). Rather, it means seeking to evangelize the person and withdrawing the privileges of church membership, such as the Lord's Supper and weekly Christian fellowship in worship. If the person is a teacher in the church and has committed grave sin or has taught gross heresy, the church should publicly rebuke him and eject him from his position. If the person repents, he should be restored to fellowship in the church (2 Cor. 2:6–11) but not necessarily to a teaching position.

As individuals, we should trust the judgment of a gospel-preaching church regarding the state of another person's soul unless there is a compelling reason to do other-wise. If a church excommunicates a person, that does not necessarily mean we cut off all contact but means that we regard the individual as someone who does not know Christ and needs to be converted through the preaching of the gospel (Matt. 18:17). The goal should always be to recover the sinner, but not at the expense of truth and holiness.

IV.

**THE GOSPEL
AND LOVE**

■ ■ ■

CHRISTIANS ARE CALLED to share the gospel and love their neighbors, and we must do so while standing firm on the truth of Scripture. This section answers questions related to how to reject falsehood and hold fast to the things of God as we seek to fulfill the Great Commission (Matt. 28:18–20; Rom. 12:9).

THE GOSPEL AND LOVE

QUESTIONS ANSWERED

I've sinned sexually. Is there hope for me?

Yes. There is always the hope of true forgiveness and restoration for those who turn from their sin and trust in the Lord Jesus Christ, even those who have committed sexual sin.

As we consider this question, we must recognize that sexual sin does have unique consequences. The Apostle Paul says, "Every other sin a person commits is outside the body, but the sexually immoral person sins against his own body" (1 Cor. 6:18). Sexual sins are not easily wiped away from our memories, nor are they easily dealt with in

"

IF WE CONFESS

OUR SINS,

HE IS FAITHFUL

AND JUST

TO FORGIVE US

OUR SINS

AND TO CLEANSE

US FROM ALL

UNRIGHTEOUSNESS.

1 JOHN 1:9

subsequent relationships. They leave a deeper scar than many other sins. For this reason, Paul urges Christians to flee sexual immorality (1 Cor. 6:18).

At the same time, the Bible offers true and full forgiveness in Christ Jesus for sexual sin. Sins committed against our own bodies have lasting consequences, but they are not unforgivable sins. For those who receive and rest upon Christ alone for salvation, sin no longer has the power to condemn (Rom. 8:1). In and through the Lord Jesus Christ, God has "forgiven us *all* our trespasses, by canceling the record of debt that stood against us with its legal demands. This he set aside, nailing it to the cross" (Col. 2:13–14, emphasis added). Whether the sexual sin is committed before one's conversion to Christ or afterward, forgiveness is available through true faith and repentance. Regardless of the severity of the sexual sin, God will in no way cast out one who comes to Him in faith with a contrite heart. God is "faithful and just to forgive us our sins and to cleanse us from *all* unrighteousness" (1 John 1:9, emphasis added). God, in His covenant grace, has bound Himself to forgive the sins of His people who confess to Him and seek forgiveness.

True repentance doesn't necessarily mean that a Christian will never fall into the same sin again, but it does entail a genuine hatred for the sin and a resolve to turn from that sin and to walk in new obedience. The Christian's relationship to sin has changed. The Christian is aware of his sin and has cast himself on the mercy of God in Christ. The Christian battles indwelling sin, but he also grieves that sin and continually turns from it to God for forgiveness and strength. There may be earthly consequences and scars for those who have fallen into grievous sin, but the permanent scars have been placed on Christ, who was wounded for the transgressions of His people. Jesus Christ promises: "All that the Father gives me will come to me, and whoever comes to me I will never cast out" (John 6:37).

What is true "compassion"?

True compassion is defined by God in His Word and is a reflection of God's character. Therefore, to know what true compassion looks like, we must understand what

"

"ALL THAT
THE FATHER
GIVES ME WILL
COME TO ME,
AND WHOEVER
COMES TO ME
I WILL NEVER
CAST OUT."

JOHN 6:37

the Bible teaches about it. Rather than being a "thing" or a "quality" that God happens to possess, compassion is God's very nature, and all human compassion originates in Him. He is "the Father of mercies and God of all comfort" (2 Cor. 1:3), and God's compassion is embodied in His Son, Jesus Christ.

Compassion has three parts. First, there is an internal dimension that involves our being moved in our hearts as we see the plight of others. This heart response includes feeling with and for others, experiencing a deep sense of their suffering and being similarly affected. This internal dimension comes to outward expression as we move to alleviate their distress with acts of beneficence or assistance, which is the second part of compassion. Compassion, therefore, is an internal movement of the heart that results in an outward movement of action on another's behalf.

The third part of compassion ensures that we are acting in a truly godly way toward others: biblical compassion is exercised *in accordance with the Word and will of God*. This last piece is critical, because many people today misunderstand compassion, even within the church. Our personal views and opinions are not the ultimate reference points of what true compassion is or how true compassion acts; God is. This means that those who advocate things such as gay marriage or the "transitioning" of transgender individuals, though they claim to be acting out of compassion, are actually twisting the true virtue of compassion because they are acting in opposition to God's Word and will. This fleshly "compassion" ultimately hurts those whom it claims to help.

Godly compassion as we interact with LGBTQ individuals means, first, that we should experience internal distress and grief as we see how sin has twisted people made in God's image and turned them into enemies of God at their core, as we were before God saved us. Before entering Jerusalem on His way to the cross, when Jesus "drew near and saw the city, he wept over it, saying, 'Would that you, even you, had known on this day the things that make for peace!'" (Luke 19:41–42). Having a heart of compassion also means that we grieve at the ways that LGBTQ people have been sinned against by others, including experiences of abuse or abandonment that have influenced their own sinful choices.

In our outward movements and actions toward LGBTQ people, compassion means that we refuse to view them with contempt or with a spirit of self-righteousness, desiring to treat them with dignity and kindness as God's image bearers. It means that we seek to be good neighbors so that they might have Christians in their lives who can reflect Christ to them (Luke 10:25–37). And true compassion means that we refuse to support their satanic deception and their rejection of God by affirming their lifestyle as an acceptable option in the eyes of God. After Jesus wept over Jerusalem, He entered the city and drove the money-changers out of the temple, refusing to affirm the perversion of God's temple (Luke 19:45–48). This will look different in various contexts, but we can have opportunities to share what we believe as we engage with LGBTQ people.

Jesus is our example as we seek to treat those around us with true, biblical compassion and love in our various relationships. Like compassion, love is defined in reference to God. Biblical love seeks what is in the best interest of others according to the Word and will of God. This is how Jesus could be filled with grace and truth, for He always sought what was in the best interest of others (grace) while also affirming that what is best is always defined by God (truth). The world tells us that "love is love," but God tells us that love "does not rejoice at wrongdoing, but rejoices with the truth" (1 Cor. 13:6).

How can I love family members and friends who are LGBTQ without compromising my Christian faith?

In all things, we are to speak the truth in love (Eph. 4:15), but rightly loving in particular situations depends on many factors. When it comes to loving LGBTQ family members and friends without compromising our Christian faith, we must apply biblical wisdom to avoid celebrating sinful lifestyles, placing others in situations that might tempt them to sin, and misleading others about what we believe.

If we are invited to a loved one's event, it is wise to ask, What is the meaning of the event, and does it celebrate the person's *life* or the person's *lifestyle*? If an event is celebrating sin or a sinful lifestyle or is somehow approving of evil or condemning what is righteous, then Christians cannot attend, because their attendance shows approval and celebration of the sin. This makes attending an LGBTQ wedding unacceptable in every case. This would also extend to events such as an LGBTQ couple's anniversary celebration. If the attendee is celebrating a non-sinful accomplishment or milestone such as a graduation, birthday, or retirement, then attendance may be acceptable.

As we seek to care about LGBTQ loved ones, it is wise to ask, Will my actions facilitate their sin? Jesus warns us not to do anything that might tempt someone else to sin (Matt. 18:7). Thus, we must take care not to place sinners in situations that will make it easier for them to transgress God's law. A practical example here is inviting a homosexual couple into one's home for dinner or an extended stay. Gathering a group together for a meal does not necessarily introduce more temptations to sin, but allowing the couple to share a bed in the guest bedroom certainly does. The former is probably acceptable in most cases, but the latter is not.

Finally, as we consider the broader context of our actions toward LGBTQ friends and family members, it is wise to ask, How will others outside my relationship with the person in question interpret my acts of love? We need to be careful with how far we take this, but Paul does talk about our duty not to cause the weaker brother to sin (Rom. 14). There are a variety of things that we can do to show love to those in a sinful lifestyle that, in and of themselves, may be acceptable but that may also be unwise in particular settings or if they include certain people. For example, attending a birthday party for a gay person may be perfectly fine, but it might not be wise to take a child there.

Jesus tells us to go the extra mile (Matt. 5:41), so Christians must be willing to go far in showing love to someone who identifies as LGBTQ. We are not to treat them as beyond all hope of redemption, be cruel to them, or otherwise treat them unjustly or unfairly (as the Bible defines those concepts). There is much that we can do and that God leaves up to our discretion, expecting us to apply biblical wisdom (Ps. 119:11). But there are lines that we may not cross, for we must not do anything that communicates approval of sin. And as we seek to love our LGBTQ family members, friends, colleagues, and acquaintances, let us remember God's provision for us in the local church, seeking help from our pastors and elders as we encounter particular situations.

How should I respond if people call me judgmental or bigoted?

When people call us judgmental or bigoted because we hold to Christian truth, we should not be surprised. We should never apologize for telling the truth and never present God's truth as our opinion, and we should remember that God promises a blessing to those who are insulted for His sake (Matt. 5:11).

The world hates the truth. It does so because it hates God. Sinful humanity is fundamentally opposed to God and His law and will do all that it can to oppose Him,

"

"BLESSED ARE
YOU WHEN OTHERS
REVILE YOU AND
PERSECUTE YOU AND
UTTER ALL KINDS
OF EVIL AGAINST
YOU FALSELY ON MY
ACCOUNT."

MATTHEW 5:11

up to and including lashing out against His people. This means that when Christians proclaim the truth of God, they will often face opposition. We see this even on the most elementary level when we say that there is only one way to be saved—through faith in Jesus Christ (John 14:6). More specifically, however, Christians will face opposition when they explain the Bible's teachings on gender and sexuality. Many people believe that saying someone's behavior is wrong is the same as condemning that person and that condemning someone is wrong. Yet we do not condemn others; only God can condemn, and we ourselves would be condemned if it weren't for the salvation that we have in Jesus Christ (Rom. 1:18; 8:34). We must be willing to bear reproach for proclaiming what we believe in truth and love (Matt. 5:44; Eph. 4:15).

When we encounter opposition, we must not apologize for holding to the truth. We are doing nothing wrong by declaring the truth of God, so we have nothing to apologize for. We must be cautious, however, that we are declaring the truth of God in a way that is respectful and that honors God, not in a way that is obnoxious or needlessly confrontational. If people are offended, the offense must come from our message and not from our manner of delivering that message. We can and should apologize if we have not acted in love when speaking the truth, but we must not apologize for telling the truth.

We ought to make clear that in declaring the truth of God, we are not merely stating our personal opinion. We can and should point to Scripture and indicate that we are merely repeating what God the Creator says to us. We should make clear that we hold to these things not because they are our ideas but because God has revealed them.

When we face opposition, as painful as it may be, we can be assured that God is pleased with our faithfulness as we strive to glorify Him with our words and actions and that we will be blessed as we suffer dishonor for His name (Matt. 5:11–12). Believers must follow the example of Christ by entrusting themselves to God when they are opposed for doing what is right and pleasing to Him. They must also be prepared to bless and pray for those who persecute them (1 Cor. 4:12; 1 Peter 2:23; 3:16).

How can Christians serve brothers and sisters in Christ who experience same-sex attraction?

Christians can serve fellow believers who experience same-sex attraction in a number of ways. This ministry will look different depending on various factors, including the strength and frequency of the attractions, the individual's attitude toward the attractions, and the individual's life circumstances. There are at least six ways that Christians can love fellow believers who experience same-sex attraction.

First, we can pray for them. We can pray for them not to give in to the desires of their flesh. This can take the form of appealing to God to strengthen them in their resolve to not nurse, act on, or in any way identify with such desires. We can pray that the Holy Spirit will continue to reveal to them the beauty and glory of Jesus Christ, that by beholding Him they would become more like Him (2 Cor. 3:18). For those who are married, prayers can be offered for the purity and honor of the marriage (Heb. 13:4). For those who do not marry, we can pray for their contentment and satisfaction with Christ.

Second, we can speak the truth in love (Eph. 4:15). This means that we do not minimize the sin or pretend that it is not sin. It is never truly loving to regard sin lightly. A faithful and repenting Christian will want to hear the faithful correction of a friend, even if it is unpleasant. It's not loving to tell someone that his desires are fine as long as he doesn't act on them. No, if it is a sin to commit acts of unrighteousness, it is also a sin to desire or be drawn to those works of unrighteousness. Calling sinful desires what they are can help Christians persevere in their battle with sin. In the throes of temptation, these loving reminders can strengthen them in their resolve to align their desires with God's revealed will.

Third, we can direct them to Christ. We should encourage them by reminding them of the ministry of intercession that the Lord Jesus Christ exercises for His people. Hebrews says that Christ has become "a merciful and faithful high priest in the service of God, to make propitiation for the sins of the people. For because he himself has suffered when tempted, he is able to help those who are being tempted" (2:17–18). Further, Jesus can sympathize with His people

"

SINCE THEN WE
HAVE A GREAT HIGH
PRIEST WHO HAS PASSED
THROUGH THE HEAVENS,
JESUS, THE SON OF GOD,
LET US HOLD FAST OUR
CONFESSION. FOR WE DO
NOT HAVE A HIGH PRIEST
WHO IS UNABLE TO
SYMPATHIZE WITH OUR
WEAKNESSES,

BUT ONE WHO IN EVERY RESPECT HAS BEEN TEMPTED AS WE ARE, YET WITHOUT SIN. LET US THEN WITH CONFIDENCE DRAW NEAR TO THE THRONE OF GRACE, THAT WE MAY RECEIVE MERCY AND FIND GRACE TO HELP IN TIME OF NEED.

HEBREWS 4:14–16

"

in their weaknesses: "Since then we have a great high priest who has passed through the heavens, Jesus, the Son of God, let us hold fast our confession. For we do not have a high priest who is unable to sympathize with our weaknesses, but one who in every respect has been tempted as we are, yet without sin. Let us then with confidence draw near to the throne of grace, that we may receive mercy and find grace to help in time of need" (4:14–16). Like all Christians, believers who experience same-sex attraction must regularly draw near to the throne of grace for help in their time of need.

Fourth, we can build relationships in which we love and welcome these believers into our lives and the lives of families in the church. Some Christians who battle same-sex attraction might not marry or have children, and as a result, they may experience a deep sense of loneliness. The church is to live as a spiritual family in which we build up one another and care for one another, seeking to ensure that no one is left to struggle alone.

Fifth, we can remind one another of the glories of heaven that await those who hold fast to their confession and persevere in faith and repentance to the end. Since there will be no more sin or tears in heaven, gazing at our future hope can empower present faithfulness as we mortify sin and pursue "the holiness without which no one will see the Lord" (Heb. 12:14). As the Apostle Peter writes, "Preparing your minds for action, and being sober-minded, set your hope fully on the grace that will be brought to you at the revelation of Jesus Christ" (1 Peter 1:13).

Finally, we can emphasize the importance of spiritual disciplines and the means of grace. The Lord has given His people means by which He nourishes their faith. The Christian who is struggling with unwanted desires should be committed to sitting under the preaching of the Word, reading Scripture, observing and partaking of the sacraments, engaging in regular prayer, and enjoying fellowship with the saints. Internal struggles can be isolating, and these Christians will be helped by our encouraging them to stay the course and submit to God's means of grace. Through these means, the Spirit renews our minds (Rom. 12:2), conforms us to Christ (Rom. 8:29), and causes our affections for Him to supplant sinful affections.

How can I share the gospel with LGBTQ people?

In many ways, sharing the gospel with LGBTQ people looks the same as sharing the gospel with anyone else. We pray for God's help, seek to help them understand that their sin and rebellion put them under God's wrath, and present Jesus Christ as their only hope for eternal life and their only ultimate hope in their struggle against their sin. God's Word diagnoses the sin of LGBTQ people and provides the solution in the gospel of Jesus Christ, just as it does for everyone else: "For all have sinned and fall short of the glory of God, and are justified by his grace as a gift, through the redemption that is in Christ Jesus" (Rom. 3:23–24).

Remember that the person you're speaking to bears God's image. For this reason, he or she must be treated with respect, not insulted or demeaned. Further, as you seek to share the gospel with an LGBTQ person, pray constantly. Pray for opportunities to share the gospel and that the Lord of the harvest would see fit to gather this person in (Luke 10:2). Remember that no one is beyond His reach. Even the Apostle Paul, who had once been a violent persecutor of the church, was saved by the sovereign grace and mighty power of God (see Gal. 1:13–16).

LGBTQ sin is sometimes thought to be unique because it goes to the level of identity. Most people don't identify themselves with their sin at the deepest level—they don't say "I am a hateful person" or "I am a lustful person" and own that identity as much as others might with "I am a gay person." While in some sense this might make LGBTQ sinners a unique evangelistic challenge, the reality is that no one apart from Christ wants to give up his sin. A sinner—whether that sin takes the form of unrighteousness or self-righteousness—will hold on to his sin whether he identifies himself with it or not, unless and until the Holy Spirit convinces him to give it up.

Therefore, one's LGBTQ status is not the central issue in his or her life, no matter how much he or she tries to make it so; the central issue is his or her status as one who is fundamentally at enmity with God and justly under His condemnation. Ephesians 2:3 tells us that "we all once lived in the passions of our flesh, carrying out the desires of the body and the mind, and were by nature children of wrath, like the rest of mankind." This broken relationship with God is evident not just in the person's life but all around us; everyone knows that something is wrong with the world. We can all even see things that are wrong in ourselves. We as Christians can help LGBTQ people understand that ultimately the cause of all that is wrong is our sin and rebellion, no matter what form it takes specifically. Once these things are understood, the cross of Christ can be presented as the solution that reconciles us to God. There is one Savior and one way of salvation for all people, regardless of the type of sin we commit, and all who trust in Christ alone for salvation can rest in the truth that "for our sake [God] made him to be sin who knew no sin, so that in him we might become the righteousness of God" (2 Cor. 5:21).

Finally, realize that it is not ultimately your job to save this person. If he or she is among God's elect, Christ has paid for the individual's sin and will draw him or her to Himself by His Spirit—perhaps with you as His instrument through your preaching of the gospel. It can be painful to watch someone live in a way that diverges from God's

"

FOR OUR SAKE

HE MADE HIM

TO BE SIN

WHO KNEW NO SIN,

SO THAT IN HIM

WE MIGHT

BECOME THE

RIGHTEOUSNESS

OF GOD.

2 CORINTHIANS 5:21

revealed will, especially when that person is a loved one. In such cases, we must strive to communicate that our counsel comes from a place of love and concern. And we must remember that our call is to be faithful and to glorify God with our words and our actions.

I feel pressure to affirm or participate in the LGBTQ lifestyle. What should I do?

Many Christians will face intense pressure to affirm or participate in the LGBTQ lifestyle, and this pressure can seem overwhelming. Even when we know that the right thing to do is not to affirm or participate in sexual sin, it can be hard for us to follow through on these convictions consistently. Even if we never affirm the sin explicitly, we might be silent on the matter where we should speak up. Yet God has not left us to face this pressure without any help. Here are some steps that we can take to resist the cultural pressure to affirm or participate in the LGBTQ lifestyle.

First, make sure that you have strong Christian friends and are in a good church where the truth of God concerning sexual matters is embraced and taught. We are social creatures who are influenced by our environment. Unless we surround ourselves with people who affirm biblical truth and put ourselves under the consistent preaching of God's Word, we will open ourselves up to giving in to the culture of sin and death on sexual matters. Good Christian fellowship and teaching will help strengthen our resolve, so we must choose our friends and churches wisely.

Second, get solidly grounded in the biblical teaching on sex and gender. This field guide is only a starting point. Study key biblical texts on the issue such as Genesis 1–2 and 1 Corinthians 6–7. Sit under sound preaching and teaching that is not afraid to deal with sex and gender when the subject arises in the biblical text.

Third, be cognizant of how media shapes our views on sexual issues. Pay attention to what you are watching, reading, and listening to, and be aware of how it might be communicating an LGBTQ-affirming agenda and undermining the truth of Scripture on these matters. Make adjustments to media consumption where necessary so that your mind is not unduly shaped by the lies of popular culture on sex and gender.

Fourth, resolve not to compromise the truth, and pray that the Lord would strengthen you to stand for Him. Ask God to help you remain firm in your commitment to the truth. Trust Him to supply the help that you need after you ask for it in prayer.

Finally, take heart. We are not the first generation to have to confront widespread untruth in the culture, and we will not be the last, unless Jesus Christ returns first. Jesus will preserve His church, and we have the privilege of being that church and shining the light of truth in this dark world. God promises to reward those who are faithful to Him. Even if we suffer for standing for the truth now, such suffering will be temporary. In eternity, God will commend us for being good and faithful servants when we uphold His truth (Matt. 25:23).